TOULOUSE-LAUTREC

FELICITAS TOBIEN

TOULOUSE-LAUTREC

Artline Editions

Translated by Stephen Gorman

©1989 by Berghaus Verlag — D 8347 Kirchdorf/Inn
English Language Rights: Artlines UK Ltd, 2 Castle Street,
Thornbury, Bristol. Avon, England
Printed in West Germany — Imprimé en Allemagne
ISBN 1 871487 25 0

Lautrec only placed his trust in people when he felt that they understood him, when he knew them for a long time or when something about them had made a special impression on him. Then even that person's social status was unimportant to him. He saw life as a painter and only thought about his art. A completely ordinary person whose hair or jacket, head or beard was, for example, unusual to him interested him much more than a well-known personality who had no special characteristics which pleased his eye. He never did anything under compulsion and therefore his only principle was pleasure. And it would have been just as difficult for him to have been friendly to someone he did not like as to have painted to order.

This of course led to him surrounding himself with the most varied and unusual people. His friends will never forget the strange gallery of live marionettes which Toulouse-Lautrec gathered.

Paul Leclercq
(from his recollections of
talks with Toulouse-Lautrec)

"The whole world knows the photographs of the little stunted man. Only his head and body had developed normally. The head looked as if it was screwed on to the sloping shoulders. A long black beard had a strange ornamental effect. Arms and legs were those of a six year old boy. But this crippled body contained an exceptional vivacity which almost surpassed Toulouse-Lautrec's spirit. His quick-witted answers — like those of a mischievous clown — were astounding. Full of brutal sensuality, his speech was sometimes uncontained, sometimes exceptionally witty and other times completely unconventional . . ." (Henry van de Velde)

What Toulouse-Lautrec lacked in physical size, was more than made up for in his artistic abilities. The "little big man", as he has often been called since his death, outgrew himself in his works and left posterity an oeuvre of considerable dimensions.

Lautrec tried — in spite of, or because of, his handicap — to find the most positive sides of life for himself. At a disadvantage because of his health and his outer appearance, he felt himself magically drawn to everything vital and beautiful and was addicted to the colourful, lively activities of the so-called demi-monde which accepted him, a scion of an old French noble family, with open arms. He undoubtedly suffered because of his abnormal appearance. Once he said, "You have to be able to suffer yourself," but just this was apparently difficult for him.

Because of his fear of being alone, he sought company and was lucky to find true friends among all those who crossed his path. However, the inner loneliness remained. In order to fight this or at least to cover it, he hid his innermost feelings behind a protective wall of self-irony and cynicism.

When Henri Marie Raymond de Toulouse-Lautrec-Monfa was born on November 24th, 1864 in the "Hôtel du Bosc", the medieval town palace of the family in Albi in southern France, no one had any idea of the insidious illness of the bones which threatened his growth.

The son of Count Alphonse Charles Jean Marie and Comtesse Adèle Zoë Marie Marquette née Tapié de Céleyran was a descendant of the counts of Toulouse, an old important noble family which can be traced back to Charlemagne.

Henri's father had in the tradition of his extravagant, idle ancestors prematurely taken off his officer's uniform and dedicated his life mainly to hunting. This and other passions led to the married couple living apart, and after the death of Henri's younger brother Richard, they separated.

The young Henri was spoiled by his quiet devout mother, both grandmothers and numerous other relatives, and at first he developed splendidly. He inflicted everyone with his happiness. "Henri sings from morning till evening. He is a real cricket," one of his grandmothers noticed happily and believed that with "such a lively boy" one did "not have to worry."

But the fact that Henri had many interests, was a passionate rider and a talented drawer, who knew how to spend his time in the family seat usefully, could not hide forever that something was not quite right with his physical development.

In 1872, the countess moved to Paris with her son where he enrolled in the Lycée Fontanes and got to know Maurice Joyant who remained a lifelong friend. Later he was executor of Lautrec's estate and his first biographer. He also founded the Toulouse-Lautrec museum in Albi.

As he did not have any problems with learning, Henri liked to occupy himself with things which he regarded as more important during his lessons. Books and exercise books were covered with caricatures of his teachers and fellow pupils as well as with sketches and drawings of animals, especially horses. The artistic talent was inherited from his ancestors who had proved themselves to be gifted amateurs for generations. His father and uncles Charles and Odon also practised drawing, modelling and painting in watercolour with skill and enthusiasm.

Henri's unstable physical condition forced a return to his hometown in 1875. It was hoped that the fresh air in the country would be instrumental in stabilizing and improving his general state of health. From then on Henri was educated by his mother and private tutors.

What no one wanted to admit in the beginning soon became a painful certainty. Lautrec suffered from a bone atrophy, a hereditary disease whose origins could probably be found in his parents blood relationship. His father and mother were first cousins.

Henri's growth was considerably limited, his legs were oversensitive and could not support him for long. But the worst was still to come.

In May 1878, when he was just thirteen years old, he fell over a low chair in such an unfortunate way that he suffered a femoral fracture in his left leg. Recovery was very slow. Courses of treatment at spas in Amélie-les-Bains, Nice and Barèges were supposed to effect a final recuperation, but he had no sooner reported to a friend, ". . . I am beginning to walk with a crutch and a person's help," than he suffered a further blow of fate, just a year after the first one. During his stay at the spa in Barèges he fractured his right thigh when he fell while walking with his mother in a dried-up streambed.

Henri suffered the pain which the protracted treatment brought with great courage. Repeated water and rest cures, electro-shock treatment of his legs and other procedures meant a hard test of patience for him, especially as hopes of a normal untroubled life slowly disappeared. "I am alone for the whole day, I read a little, but when I do it for too long, I get headaches. I draw and paint as much as I am able to without getting tired, and when it begins to get dark, I ask myself whether Jeanne d'Armagnac (a cousin) will come to my bedside. Sometimes she comes and wants to play with me, and I listen to her when she speaks without being able to look at her directly. She is so tall and beautiful! And I am neither tall nor beautiful."

It was unusual for him to utter such melancholy words, he mostly tried to appear composed and gay, and in many of his letters and diary entries he developed a sort of grim humour. For instance, in late summer 1879 he confided to his friend Étienne Devismes, ". . . On Monday the surgical crime was complete, and such a wonderful fracture from a surgical point of view (definitely not mine!) saw daylight. The doctor was fascinated and left me in peace until this morning. This morning he left me under the false pretence that I should sit up straight, bend my leg at right angles and suffer terribly . . ." In spite

8

Table I

Ambassadeurs: Aristide Bruant (Poster). 1892
Colour lithograph, 133.8 × 91.7 cm

of the sarcastic comments it is not difficult to read between the lines how the boy suffered, that not only had he to come to terms with the fact that the fractures healed very slowly and inadequately, but also that his leg had completely stopped growing and that he would remain small.

"I am small, but I am not a dwarf," he later said, when faced with an even smaller man who he often saw — with obvious satisfaction — on the Montmartre.

The only thing which was able to give Lautrec consolation and strength in this difficult time was drawing and painting. ". . . I am now obsessed by painting," he wrote to Étienne Devismes on February 11th, 1880, "my room is full of things which do not even deserve to be called daubs. But it helps to pass the time . . ."

From this pastime an art developed which rapidly matured. "I have set myself the task of being honest and not idealizing," the sixteen year old commented, "Perhaps that is a mistake, but I find it impossible to overlook warts: I love to decorate them with mischievous little hairs, to make them even bigger than they are and to place a shining point on them." A fundamental to which he remained true.

After Henri had passed his final exams at the second attempt, he decided to become a painter and went to Réné Princeteau in Paris, a deaf and dumb animal painter who was friendly with Henri's father. He had already given the youth a lot of valuable advice. In 1914, Princeteau remembered his time with Lautrec, ". . . He came into my studio every morning: in '78, when he was fourteen years old, he copied my studies and painted my portrait, although I shuddered with horror. During the holidays he painted from nature, portraits, horses, dogs and soldiers on manoeuvres. In winter, in Cannes he painted ships, the sea and riders. Henri and I went together to the circus because of the horses and to the theatre for the decorations. He knew a lot about horses and dogs."

There existed a cordial unterstanding between pupil and tutor. A love of animals, painting and last but not least their individual destinies united them in a very special way.

The young nobleman was interested in everything that moved because his movement was so limited through his handicap. He knew that he would only play an active role in life with his art and would only be able to duplicate the motions which his legs were incapable of with paintbrush and pencil.

Among the numerous paintings and drawings which were created before the time when Lautrec officially began to study there were already small masterpieces. In some pictures there was a touch of Impressionism which leads us to believe that the works of the Impressionists must have been known to him.

Princeteau, as an experienced and responsible artist, soon recognized that Lautrec needed a different type of tuition than he was able to offer if his talent was to unfold completely. He therefore sent him to Léon Bonnat who was one of the most famous artists in France in those days. Lautrec was very proud to be accepted as a pupil by Bonnat in April 1882, but this joy was short-lived as a few months later Bonnat accepted a position in the École des Beaux-Arts and did not think of taking Lautrec with him. The reason for this was that he underestimated Lautrec's drawing abilities or deliberately closed his eyes to them. "Your painting is not at all bad," he said, ". . . but your drawing is absolutely awful . . ." Even later, when Lautrec had proved himself in the whole world, his former teacher did not revise his negative opinion; on the contrary, he at first was responsible for hindering works by Lautrec coming into the Louvre after Lautrec had died.

When Bonnat had dismissed all of his pupils, Toulouse-Lautrec moved to the studio of Fernand Cormon in September 1882. He was a young, but very well-known Salon painter. Lautrec described him as "a powerful, austere and original talent."

Cormon was a liberal man who hardly used his authority and who did not attempt to force his pupils into any kind of stereotyped academic pattern. Lautrec retained his individuality and Cormon respected this. His tuition did not have a notable influence on the development of the young count anyway. Lautrec wrote in a letter on February 10th, 1883, ". . . Cormon's corrections are much more friendly than Bonnat's. He looks at everything which you show him and greatly encourages you . . . but actually I like that less! The whiplashes of my old patron were sharp, and I did not protect myself. Here I am a little weakened and need courage to make a careful drawing where a worse one would be just as good in Cormon's eyes anyway. But for the last two weeks he is more alert and has brought a few pupils up to the mark, including me. . ."

Lautrec was exceptionally ambitious and preferred to visit exhibitions in his spare time. He gave himself no peace and just wanted to learn diligently and do something which he could be proud of, as art was the best means of self-realization for him. It distracted him from his sad fate, he found a joy in living through it. With art he counterbalanced his inferiority complex. The older he became, the more his stunted body stood out and his facial expressions became less attractive. "He never blamed anyone although he suffered a lot because of his appearance. People turned away from him, but generally more in sympathy than in derision." (Alphonse de Toulouse-Lautrec)

Lautrec often had to suffer other people's thoughtlessness. He was called "the gnome with a child's legs", "shorty" or suffered even more hurtful descriptions. Only those who knew him closer appreciated him. They did not see the cripple in him but rather the ingenious, amusing human being, and they recognized that behind what the others so quickly called horrible, values were concealed which counted more than any ideals of beauty.

In Cormon's studio, Lautrec became friendly with his fellow students Henri Rachou, Adolphe Albert, Émile Bernard, François Gauzi, René Grenier and Louis Anquetin. At Cormon's, he also got to know Vincent van Gogh with whom he also became friendly. The portrait of van Gogh which Lautrec painted in pastel in 1887 belongs to the most fascinating early works. In spite of its unpretentiousness and unobtrusiveness the picture is able to convey the Dutchman's personality to the observer in an incomparable fashion.

Lautrec lived until 1884 with his mother in her Parisian flat, after which he moved to friends on the Montmartre. In 1886 he finished his studies with Cormon and rented himself his own studio in the Rue Tourlaque so that he could in future work as a self-employed artist.

After he had loosened the family ties a little, he gradually began to settle into an environment which from his relatives point of view was anything other than befitting his social position. The change was not easy for him, and he admitted to his grandmother, "I have to make a lot of effort because — and you know it as well as I do — I lead the life of a true Bohemian against my will; I do find it very difficult to acclimatize myself in such a milieu. Admittedly one of the main reasons why I do not feel happy on Montmartre is that I am burdened with a great deal of sentimental ties which I must rid myself of completely if I am to achieve anything at all."

But with time he discovered the benefits which developed for him as an artist from this new style of living and so Montmartre, with everything that belonged to it, became a second home to him. Lautrec observed, sketched and painted with a great deal of intuition as if he had never experienced anything but this milieu. He got to know the people's problems and needs, saw stars rising and fading in the cabaret heaven and found an inexhaustible source of inspiration for his work.

He was soon a welcome guest in cafés, cabarets and dancehalls. In the "Moulin Rouge" he had more or less belonged to the living inventory since its opening in 1889. A table was reserved for him there every evening, and it seldom remained empty. In the foyer hung his "Trick Rider in Circus Fernando" (1888) and later also "Dance in the Moulin Rouge" (1892).

It is said that the environment forms the person; in a painter's case it also forms his work. Lautrec is probably the best example for this. In his beginnings he preferred to represent horses and riders, but now he revelled in everything that Parisian night life had to offer his artistic eye: dance, theatre, circus and brothel. He became the interpreter and chronicler of this small world where, it must be added, man in his individuality always remained in the forefront for him.

A great many Parisian cabaret stars from those days can thank him for their popularity. They would have long ago faded into obscurity if Lautrec had not made them immortal through his paintings and posters. La Goulue (the glutton), Yvette Guilbert, Jane Avril, Aristide Bruant, Valentin le Désossé (Valentin the snake man) and all the others felt honoured by the interest which he showed them even if his form of representation was sometimes deliberately overdone and therefore not exactly flattering to them.

In 1894 the chanson singer Yvette Guilbert pleaded with the artist who had, among other things, dedicated albums of lithographs to her, in one of her numerous letters, ". . . But for heaven's sake don't make me so awfully horrible! A bit less. . . ! Several people have let out wild cries at my home when they saw the coloured sketch. . . Not everyone just sees the artistic side. . ."

He completely ignored landscape painting, the preferred province of countless colleagues, apart from a few early works, for example, "In the Fields" (1880), "At the River Bank in Céleyran" (1880) and "Pinegrove in Céleyran" (1880).

"Only the figure exists," he categorically stated, "the landscape is nothing more and should be nothing more than an ingredient: the pure landscape painter is a brute. The landscape should only serve to make the personality of a figure more tangible. Corot is only great in his figures, the same is true of Millet, Renoir and Whistler. When figure painters represent a landscape, they handle it like a face; Degas's landscapes are outrageous because they are dream landscapes: those from Carrière are like human masks. Monet would be even greater if he had not neglected the figures so much."

Lautrec attempted quite early to have his works exhibited. "That is the only way to draw attention to yourself," he commented, but in the beginning he had too little confidence in his ability to use his own name and therefore used various pseudonyms for a time, such as "Tréclau" or "Tolau-Segroeg".

The first collective exhibition in which he took part was in Pau in 1884. This was followed by others in 1887 which he organized together with colleagues in cafés and restaurants. He also participated in an exhibition in Toulouse.

In the meantime the Belgian group of artists "Les Vingt" had become aware of him, and Theo van Rysselberghe, one of the members, wrote towards the end of 1887, "The small, shortlegged chap is not bad at all. The fellow has talent! Definitely for the XX. . . He produces very amusing things at the moment: Circus Fernando, whores and all that. He knows a lot of people. With one word, the right sorts! He found the thought of being represented with the XX with several scenes from the Rue de Séze and the Rue Laffitte very chic."

In February 1888, Lautrec had his first joint exhibition with "Les Vingt" which was followed by others in the coming years so that now the international art market began to take notice of the young Frenchman.

Lautrec had already found regional fame when some sketches of his had been published in magazines in 1886. Theo van Gogh — Vincent van Gogh's brother — who ran the Galerie Goupil in those days, supported his works by organizing exhibitions and buying paintings from him or taking them on commission. When Maurice Joyant, his school-friend, became head of the gallery in 1890, Lautrec also had an enthusiastic supporter and patron in this judicious man.

While artists such as van Gogh, Gauguin and others recognized and praised the talent of their aristocratic colleague with absolutely no sign of envy, there were among the critics some who insisted with a naivete which bordered on maliciousness that "his colours are dirty; horrible creatures emerge from them, ghosts of vice and poverty. . ." (La Vie Artistique, Paris 1891)

But eventually such judgements were proved to be falsehoods by more objective and sensitive critics. On March 30th, 1891, O. Mirbeau reported in "L'Echo de Paris" after a collective exhibition by the "Impressionists and Symbolists" at "Le Barc de Batteville", "Toulouse-Lautrec studies the physiognomy with a substantial, spiritual and tragic power. It also gives him the ability to penetrate the character. . .", and after the first larger exhibition in 1893 in "L'Art Nouveau", "We have not seen an artist who is as talented as Toulouse-Lautrec for a long time. With him the acumen of analysis is integrated with the precision of expressive means. . . He is not bound to any school, he does not belong to any guild conventicle: detached from any influence he became his own untarnished self."

Gustave Geffroy had a similar opinion. He wrote in the newspaper "La Justice", "Toulouse-Lautrec presents himself in a style which he has created himself, which he has logically developed from the rules that are within him. . . posters such as Bruant, La Goulue and recently the Divan Japonais have conquered the streets with irrestistible power. . . The painter Lautrec becomes perfect when he comprehends how a person

Table II

Jane Avril (Poster). 1893
Colour lithograph, 120.8 × 88.5 cm

stands up, spontaneously takes a pose, moves, walks like a woman, how a dancer turns. . .''

In fact Lautrec did rush through an artistic development for which others would have needed years. His secret was that he kept himself detached from anything which stood in the way of his individuality and never allowed himself to be drawn along by any particular direction of style. Although elements of Impressionism, Neo-Impressionism, Symbolism and Art Nouveau can be traced in his works, they are not allowed to develop completely.

Besides van Gogh, Manet, Renoir and Cézanne, Lautrec especially admired Degas whose thematic choice was closest to his own.

Degas countered the admiration which the thirty year younger Lautrec had for him with haughtiness, irony and insincerity. When he spoke with Lautrec personally, he payed him compliments which had very little conviction and which always evoked nagging doubts in Lautrec's mind.

When Degas spoke with others about Lautrec, he used the opportunity to run him down. ''He wears my clothes, but cut to fit him,'' was one of his biting comments which was a play on words regarding Lautrec's art and his size. As he obviously lacked human greatness and was known to be a misanthropist perhaps nothing other than ill-will could be expected from him.

The different attitudes to life of both painters led to the different representation of the same subjects. Lautrec tended to paint more vividly and effectively so that Cézanne, when once asked about Degas, answered laconically, ''I prefer Lautrec.''

Japanese coloured woodcuts held a special fascination for the artist. He possibly had closer contact with them through van Gogh. The study of this Far Eastern art form had the result that Lautrec turned more intensively towards lithography in the last decade of his life and discovered a means of expression for himself which helped him to fame and honour even more than his painting and drawing.

In summer 1891 he received a commission from Charles Zidler, the impressario of the ''Moulin Rouge'' to make an advertisement poster for his establishment. It was an interesting task, but also a great challenge as the present poster came from the hand of Jules Chéret, an unchallenged master in the area of poster art which thanked him for its evergrowing popularity.

Lautrec gladly accepted the challenge and used all of his ambition to create something completely new and unconventional with originality. Technically he leant on the experience of his predecessor, as this offered an excellent basis which he could build on.

The ''Moulin Rouge'' poster, which has Valentin the Snake Man in the foreground, La Goulue in the middle of the picture and in the background, silhouette-like, like shadows, lots of spectators, is, even if it appears a spontaneous work of art, the result of a laborious process, as Lautrec first of all tested the motif in charcoal and in portrait studies before he ventured near the lithographic stone.

He used ''in this first printing work the paintbrush and also lithographic chalk (in the dancer's hair). However, above all the use of a spray technique, where, with the help of a brush containing paint, very small particles of colour are sprayed onto the stone through a sieve, carried out in various stages, allowed nuances and mixtures of colour of considerable abundance: for example with the figure in the foreground the colours black, red and blue are sprayed on top of each other in such a way that a dark violet was created. . ." (Götz Adriani)

The large format work opened Lautrec unimagined possibilities of design, and he awaited the appearance of his first poster with suspense, ". . . there have been a few delays with the printing," he wrote to his mother in Albi, "but it has been fun. I had a feeling of authority over my whole studio which was new to me."

In October the time had come. The "Moulin Rouge" poster was "hung on Paris's walls," and its creator became famous overnight. Lautrec had done a magnificent job with which he set standards — for himself, his contemporaries and posterity.

Others who were convinced of the publicity appeal of such a masterpiece also wanted to profit from his art, and so he received a great deal more commissions of this type within a short time. All in all he created 31 posters; those for the dancer Jane Avril, the chanson singer and cabaret owner Aristide Bruant, the ballad singer May Belfort and the dancer May Milton and for "Divan Japonais" and the "Jardin de Paris" are among the most famous.

The critics were filled with praise. Even Félix Fénéon, the keen supporter of Neo-Impressionism, did not hold back his admiration in the anarchistic publication "Père Peinard". "The devil take him, this Lautrec. He is shameless," he wrote on April 30th, 1893. "He makes no fuss concerning his drawings or his colours. White, black, red in big areas, that is his method. There will never be another one like him who portrays the grimaces of the senile capitalists as he does. How they sit at tables, in the company of little whores who lick their faces to make them hot. . . what Lautrec has plotted on posters. . . bubbles over with intention, impertinence and malevolence. . ."

Lautrec had not just conquered the art scene in Montmartre but also in Paris. At barely thirty years old, he was already a well-known personality. This appealed to his vanity especially as women — attracted by his popularity — did not hesitate in bestowing their favours on him.

He was especially attracted to several of his models, for example Suzanne Valadon, Maurice Utrillo's mother, who had also posed for Puvis de Chavannes and Renoir and who later became a painter herself, and Jane Avril, the dancer. But these relationships came to grief just the same as others which he is said to have had.

He longed for true love which he never found because he sought it in a milieu where there was naturally no room for lasting feelings. Instead of realizing this he blamed his outer appearance and said resignedly, "I would like to see the woman on this planet who has a lover who is uglier than me."

Lautrec was a cynic who, especially when he felt hurt, cheated or used, churned out his irreverent, frivolous and sometimes vulgar platitudes like little poisoned arrows. However, in his heart he was very sensitive, he just did not want to show anyone this side of his character if possible. In some of his works he unmasked himself — whether con-

sciously or unconsciously. Pictures such as the portrait of Jane Avril are at the same time a mirror of his soul. The closer he knew someone, the more he allowed his own feelings, his admiration, his reverence or his affection to flow into their painting, unless of course he meant to caricature them.

In autumn 1891 Lautrec's cousin Gabriel Tapié de Céleyran came from Lille to Paris to continue his medical studies. Lautrec also portrayed him: "Dr. Tapié de Céleyran in the Foyer of the Comédie Française" (1894). Through his cousin, Lautrec was given an insight into the clinical area and was even allowed to watch the famous surgeon Dr. Jules-Émile Péan operate. The results of such observations were the paintings "Doctor Péan Performing a Tracheotomy" (1891) and "Doctor Péan Operating" (1891).

Friendship meant a lot to Lautrec, and as he was amusing, helpful and generous, he was generally well-liked. "He grows with every encounter. In the end he seems to be more than medium-sized," the poet Jules Renard, who was the same age as Lautrec, noted in his diary.

In order to be together with his friends, Lautrec also accepted inconveniences. While he mostly used a carriage as otherwise his legs hurt more than usual when walking, he uncomplainingly joined his friends when they set out for walks in the surrounding countryside even though he could only move with a lot of effort using his walking-stick. "I waddle like a duck, but at least I'm walking!" he said.

No matter how much he enjoyed ridiculing himself and others, his sarcasm was always struck dumb by art. "It always moves me how Lautrec changes his tone when art is being discussed," his painter colleague Edouard Vuillard commented, "The man who was so cynical at every other opportunity and who talked in a risqué manner, always became completely earnest. It was like a religious belief to him."

Lautrec, who undoubtedly had a profound range of knowledge, did not appreciate it when paintings were analysed and therefore could not be persuaded to comment on his own works in public. "You don't need an explanation, look for your own," he rigourously protested when asked such questions.

But when it was said that some of his paintings appeared unfinished, he became annoyed and felt misunderstood. He admitted to his cousin Gabriel, "People annoy me. They want me to complete the thing. But I see them like that and paint them like that. . . Nothing is easier than finishing paintings in an outer sense. When you do this you lie most skillfully."

The artist was well-known for his exceptionally keen observational skills. He used most of his time carefully studying physiognomy and making notes and sketches which served as a memory aid when he was transferring what he had seen onto cardboard, wood, canvas or other materials. He missed no detail which could help towards illustrating the character. He always captured the moment in his pictures.

". . . Lautrec does not translate what he sees with the precission of a photographer but instead he interprets his impression exactly as he feels it at that moment. Every one of his sketches has the sense of a fundamental statement or a roguish piece of information. One meets the whole Lautrec in the smallest pencil stroke. . ."

The poet Paul Leclercq knew what he was talking about. He had experienced the painter at close range when Lautrec had made a masterly portrait of him in 1897 — at a point just before his physical breakdown. Leclercq came to pose three to four times a week for a month, but for no more than two or three hours per sitting.

"As soon as I entered, he asked me to take up the prearranged pose in a big wicker chair, and he placed himself in front of his easel wearing the small felt hat which he always wore in his studio. Then he directed his pince-nez at me, squinted his eyes, took his paintbrush and after having looked closely at me, he made a few light strokes in thinned down colour. While he was painting he did not speak a single word, but instead he appeared to be eating something tasty behind his moist lips, then he began to sing the 'Chanson du Forgeron' (an old obscene French song), put his paintbrush to the side and declared resolutely 'Enough work! The weather is too nice!'. . . (Paul Leclercq, 1921).

While Lautrec preferred to work in an enclosed space, he was drawn to nature in his spare time . The sea held a great attraction for him. He loved swimming or rowing with friends, and in the summer months of 1897 he even undertook a sailing tour through the Dutch canals together with the painter, engraver and stage-designer Maxime Dethomas.

Apart from Holland, Spain, Belgium and England also belonged to the artist's favourite destinations. Of course he also travelled often within his homeland France. He enjoyed staying in Arcachon and Toussat-les-Bains.

As he looked down on landscape painting and regarded himself as "completely ungifted" in this field there are unfortunately very few documents such as "The Passenger from Cabin 54" (1896) which point to his active travels.

In the two decades of his artistic production, he created innumerable designs, sketches and drawings, more than 600 paintings, around 350 lithographs, 31 posters and also 9 dry point etchings and several monotypes.

Lautrec gained fame during his lifetime primarily with his posters, while his other lithographic creations found less resonance with the public and the press. Today, however, he is regarded as one of the most brilliant graphic artists in the history of art which thanks him for considerable discoveries in the field of colour lithography. What a change in tastes can be seen when one considers that towards the end of the 19th century especially the colour lithographs, which Lautrec was one of the first to cultivate, were often a stumbling block. For example, a critic for the journal "Le Temps" criticized on November 5th, 1898, "In my humble opinion lithographers too often lose themselves in the search for effects which do not belong to the area of lithography. They are above all obsessed and infatuated with transfering their fantasies into colour: I find this obsession deplorable. In colour lithography it is impossible to achieve anything but very gaudy effects which work wonders on a poster, but just irritate and maltreat the eye in a carefully prepared print meant for an amateur's portfolio or for an album."

Although the artist said of himself that he "has always been a pencil", he always knew how to use a paintbrush with finesse; sometimes his handling of the brush was not unlike that of a pencil. Pictures such as "Model in the Studio: Héléne Vary" (1888), "Sit-

Table III

Divan Japonais (Poster). 1893
Colour lithograph, 80,8 × 60.8 cm

ting Woman with Gloves: Mademoiselle Honorine Platzer'' (1891), ''Jane Avril Leaving the 'Moulin Rouge' ''(1892) or ''Monsieur Boileau in the Café'' (1893) could be regarded as perfectly ''drawn'' paintings because of the brushstrokes which are very striking to the eye.

At the beginning of the 1890's Lautrec obtained a very unusual commission which caused him occasionally to exchange his studio and flat with an establishment in the Rue d'Amboise which was regarded as being very luxurious in the field of pleasures of the flesh.

''I spend my time in the brothel,'' he proudly declared after the owner had asked him to paint a salon which was furnished in the style of Louis XVIII. Apart from the artistic appeals, this task interested him in other ways as he always enjoyed a bit of fun, and it seems that he was well rewarded for his work on the sixteen medals with the prostitutes' faces. ''I do not feel more at home anywhere else,'' he decided and did not hesitate in widening his sphere of activity. In the course of the following years — until 1896 — he also made regular working visits to the brothels in the Rue des Moulins and the Rue Joubert. In this way a variety of pictures and sketches were created of this milieu from the viewpoint of a neutral observer without injuring the bourgeois moral standards. Among the most famous are ''In the Salon of the Rue des Moulins'' (1894), ''Rue des Moulins: The Doctor's Visit'' (1894) and ''The Sofa'' (1894).

If ''Monsieur Henri le peintre'' was extraordinarily popular with the ''ladies'', it is because of the fact that he treated them with the utmost respect, had an open ear for their problems and proved to be a reliable friend who did not misuse the trust which they placed in his artistic discretion.

Lautrec on his part was impressed to find an atmosphere of harmony in such a disreputable place, and he recognized that the girls were better than their reputation. ''They have a good heart. True refinement comes from the heart and that is enough for me. . .''

Their uncomplicated, natural ways fascinated him. ''The professional model is always like a dummy, those there, they live. . . I wouldn't dare give them 100 sous for posing, and God knows, they are worth it. They sprawl on the settees like animals. . . They have absolutely no pretentions. . .''

This unconstraint can also be seen in the prints from the colour lithography portfolio ''Elles'' which was issued by Gustave Pellet in Paris in 1896 with an edition of 100 copies. In this series Lautrec described everyday life in the ''Maisons closes''. He observed the prostitutes washing, combing their hair, dressing, eating breakfast and observing themselves critically in the mirror. The thing he respectfully withheld was their day to day occupation, and still there were critical voices who described the discrete representations as ''filth''.

How the artist wished to understand, perhaps more than others, the emotional lives of the 'ladies who measured up to his standards' as he called the harlots, can be seen in a series of pictures such as ''In Bed: The Kiss'' (1892) and ''The Two Girlfriends'' (1894 and 1895). They go beyond the scope of the usual brothel scenes as in them — free from pornographic crudeness — is clearly expressed with psychological intuition the need for tenderness. This need which they dispensed with when dealing with the paying customers is shown in the affection which they had for each other. Lautrec kept these works hidden until he died. Only his best friends were allowed to see them.

From 1893 his interest for the theatre increased, and he never tired of seeing a performance up to twenty times: He did not concentrate on the text or acting, but was more concerned with certain poses or characteristics of the performing actors.

Circus, horse-racing and bicycle-racing also held a similar fascination for him. Here he found a great deal of motifs. For his poster "La Chaîne Simpson" (1896) which he made on commission for the English bicycle and chain manufacturer Simpson, he accompanied "a bike-racing team which had to defend its title on the other side of the Channel" in London, as he wrote to his mother in June.

The artist's dissolute lifestyle had an effect on his health. A syphilis infection which he had contracted in 1888 caused him a great deal of trouble for the rest of his life.

But his zest for life was unquenchable. With no consideration of his weak constitution he exploited his strength ruthlessly and ignored all good advice and warnings which he was given. The more ardently he reached out his hand to life, the more it slipped away from him. He sought comfort in alcohol and did not see that exactly that was his enemy. The results were disastrous.

His first attack of delirium tremens came over him in 1897 during a recuperative holiday in Villeneuve-sur-Yonne. It was the beginning of the end, as, instead of controlling himself, Lautrec directed his life into even more chaotic ways and his friends became "helpless witnesses of the death struggle of a creative artist ruining himself. . . who was driven from life in a genuine suicide, in self-destruction and final decline." (Maurice Joyant)

When Lautrec's mother travelled from Paris to Albi in 1899 to care for her own mother, he completely lost his hold. He increasingly suffered from attacks of frenzy, anxiety, neurosis, depression and persecution complex. He withdrew from his friends because he did not want to listen to their warnings. He did not notice that his weakness was being shamelessly used by prostitutes and drinking mates.

At the end of February he had another breakdown and was admitted to a private mental hospital. After a radical detoxication cure came the rude awakening as he feared that he would have to remain locked up in the hospital forever. He complained to his father in a letter. "Papa, you have the opportunity to act humanely. I am locked up, but everything which is locked up dies!" With this he was reminding his father of a dedication which he had written in a book about falconry, but the cry for help went unheard.

The mother and the old friends, especially Joyant, cared for the patient. "At the end of a narrow, low corridor, in two small tiled cells, with bars on the windows, of which one was his room and the other his nurse's room, a clear-sighted Lautrec met me, already with crayons and drawings, like a liberator, like someone who again makes contact with the outside world, but full of anxiety that. . . he could be locked up there forever." (Maurice Joyant)

As the doctors would not agree to his release, Lautrec contemplated a way out. "Send me grained stones and a box of watercolours with sepia, paintbrush, lithographic chalk and good-quality ink and paper. . .," he asked of Joyant on March 17th and explained to him on his next visit, "When I have produced a certain amount of drawings, they will not be able to keep me here. I want to get away from here, they have no right to keep me."

After receiving the materials which he had requested, Lautrec immediately began working on his plan. While he created a series of chalk, ink and crayon drawings with the circus as a theme so that he would again seem to be "normal" in everybody's eyes, news of his stay in the mental hospital spread like wildfire, and several members of the press satisfied their lust for sensation with unpleasant campaigns against him and his art. For example, A. Hepp wrote in "Le Journal" on March 20th, 1899, "Toulouse-Lautrec had to land in a mental hospital . . . From now on the paintings, drawings and posters are officially signed by the unmasked madness which had previously remained anonymous."

In order to take the wind out of the sails of such smear campaigns, the art critic Arsène Alexandre, a friend of the artist, published in "Le Figaro" a counterrepresentation on March 30th, 1899, entitled "A Recuperation": ". . . My mind was set at rest and I would like to set other minds at rest. I saw an incredibly reasonable madman, an alcoholic who does not drink anymore, a lost soul who has never looked better. . ."

On the following day the doctors reached a similar opinion as Lautrec in the course of a long interview had shown "not a single sign of restlessness, excitement or mental depression." However, they felt it was necessary to keep the patient under control for a while yet.

On May 17th, it was eventually decided that he could leave the hospital, as long as a trusted person remained close to him in future to avoid the danger of a relapse. Happy to "escape prison", Lautrec agreed. "I bought my freedom with my drawings," he now told everyone he met.

Paul Viaud, a distant relative from Bordeaux, took over the responsible task of protecting Lautrec from a life of debauchery and the dangers of alcohol. Half roguishly, half disrespectfully, Lautrec enjoyed introducing him as "my elephant driver, a ruined man of the world."

At first it seemed that the artist was more energy laden than before his breakdown. Together with Viaud he undertook extensive journeys to Le Crotoy, Le Havre, Arcachon, Fabre, Taussat and Marlromé which were mainly meant to serve his recovery but which were at the same time used by him for his work — in the exuberance of his joy in his regained freedom.

Maurice Joyant commissioned the portrait "Miss Dolly the English Woman from the 'Star' in Le Havre" (1899). There is an oil painting as well as a red-chalk drawing of this, both of which are today in the Musée Toulouse-Lautrec in Albi.

The artistic aspect gained importance in Lautrec's later works. In pictures such as "The Milliner" (1900), "In the 'Rat Mort' " (ca. 1899/1900) and in the pictures mentioned above, the brushstrokes seem strong and balanced and give no hint of the physical decline of the painter.

As soon as his strength waned again, Lautrec again reached for the bottle. So that Viaud would not suspect him, he obtained a special walking stick which could be screwed apart to reveal a hollow inside. In this secret "brandy bottle" he could inconspicuously carry his emergency supply. But as Lautrec's dependance on alcohol became increasingly greater and he was unable to work without drinking, it was soon at an end with the secretiveness — around the turn of the century. He drank in public, and neither Viaud nor others were able to persuade him to stop his alcoholic excesses.

Lautrec's will to live had been broken. The only thing to which he still clung was his work, although it demanded the utmost in strength and concentration from him. For the portrait "Maurice Joyant in the Somme Bay" which he painted in 1900 during a trip which he made together with his friend in the Bay of Arcachon, he is said to have required seventy sittings.

At the beginning of December in this year, Lautrec rented a flat and studio in Bordeaux where he intended to spend the winter. Again he allowed himself to be swept away by his enthusiasm for theatre, for people and movement, one more time he attempted to capture life with his eyes and to record it in his pictures. It was like a last flicker.

In the Grand Théâtre in Bordeaux at this time, Jacques Offenbach's operetta "The Lovely Helena" and the opera "Messalina" from Isidore de Lara were on the programme. Lautrec was very taken by the performances and did not hesitate writing to Joyant. "My dear Maurice, do you have — good or bad — photos of Lara from 'Messalina'? This piece claims my full attention, but the more I am informed over it, the better it is . . .''

It can be assumed that his friend complied with this request. In any case Lautrec created a series of six paintings based on "Messalina", two lithographs on "Lovely Helena" and drawings based on both works.

However, spring again brought a breakdown which forced him to rest. On March 31st, 1901, he informed Joyant, "I feed myself by vomiting: the way is also blocked for Bacchus and Venus . . .''

As Lautrec guessed that he would not live much longer, he travelled to Paris in April 1901 to bring his affairs in order, to sign paintings and sketches and to bid his friends farewell. His last two lithographs were made in this period, "Jouets de Paris, Couverture" and "Zamboula-Polka", both commissioned works for Paul Leclercq and Désiré Dihau.

On July 15th, he left the city and travelled to the sea with Paul Viaud. Although his strength waned more and more, he carried on painting untiringly until he suffered a stroke in the middle of August in Taussat which left him paralysed on one side.

He sought refuge with his mother in Malromé Castle. Her care and the inner affection which bound him to her offered the dying man comfort and security. When Lautrec seemed to be feeling a little better, he threw himself into his work again. The picture which he began was intended as a wall decoration for a room in the castle and portrayed Paul Viaud in the uniform of an admiral from the 18th century.

Table IV

May Milton (Poster). 1895
Colour lithograph, 79.5 × 61 cm

It is incomprehensible that the small, completely exhausted Lautrec chose to work on such a large format painting at this point in time — it measures 139 x 153 cm. But the artist involved himself completely in this work, it was "his last pleasure" as he told his doctor who forbade him to paint before "The Admiral Viaud" was completed.

A photograph, taken around the end of August 1901, is a disturbing document of the frailty of Lautrec who was not yet 37 years old. An "old " man sits in his chair, exhausted and lost in his own thoughts. He has crossed his feet on a footstool, his hands hang weakly to the front. It can be seen that he has done with life.

"I know that I must die," Lautrec admitted to his mother in the first days of September. "Just a few weeks ago I did not want to admit that I was dying. I was afraid to shock you too much with the thought. But now you have realized it yourself. And so everything is alright . . ."

The loyal Paul Viaud accompanied the artist to the end of his way, and corresponding to the dying man's wishes his friend and cousin Gabriel Tapié de Céleyran came from Paris. On September 8th, Lautrec's father Count Alphonse also arrived at Malromé Castle. When Lautrec saw him, his sarcasm showed once more. He mocked, "I knew that you would not miss the death halloo, Papa."

With the words, "Mama, just you. Dying is damned hard!" he died in the early hours of September 9th, 1901. His life had been a heavy burden, but he had loved it in spite of that.

On the following day his obituary appeared in the "Journal de Paris": "A name, a master who died prematurely: one of the few who seize and send a shiver through you. As a wealthy person he was able to free himself of all the hardships of living and dedicate himself to an observation of life. What he saw is not very favourable for the last turn of the century whose true painter he was. He sought reality, despising fiction or chimera which falsify ideas by unbalancing the spirits . . . He was content to look. He did not see like many others what we seem to be, he saw what we are. And then he showed us ourselves with a certainty of brushstroke and at the same time with a gentle and certain boldness . . . He did not just want to make a piece of art, he revealed himself to be a deep, powerful psychologist. His teachings are sad but true. And therefore there remains to the master of the painters an epoch which we do not know, because we have sometimes lived through it as sceptics and certainly almost always as uncaring and uninvolved people."

As opposed to this laudatory article many obituaries served as a denigration of the artist. It is "lucky for mankind that there are only a few artists of his kind" appeared in a newspaper, and in the same article a "wicked talent" and "corruptive and deplorable influence" were also mentioned. Another critic even dared to declare that Lautrec's work "killed him", it "murdered him". How short-sighted contemporaries can be!

Short-sightedness was also partly responsible for the fact that the relationship between Lautrec and his father was always rather tense. The count found it difficult to accept that the proud family from which he came was pulled down to the cheap level ot the Montmartre by his son, and therefore it was impossible for him to understand the world of his son's paintings. He found what was represented on the pictures of no use to anyone, felt it was "too carelessly worked out" and "made with an axe". In his eyes the surroundings in which his son lived were no starting point for true works of art.

On October 22nd, 1901, Count Alphonse de Toulouse-Lautrec-Monfa transfered his rights to his son's legacy to Henri's schoolfriend Maurice Joyant. ". . . I am not playing at being generous," he wrote, "when I surrender all my paternal rights to you, if what our dear departed has made can be called an inheritance. Your brotherly friendship has already long replaced my slack influence so that — if you wish — you can continue to play this amiable role, just for the satisfaction of your heart which was always full of goodness for your schoolfriend. I do not intend to change my opinion, and now — because he is dead — to praise to the skies something which I could not see as anything else but impertinent, brazen studio studies on cardboard during his lifetime. — Alphonse de T.-L."

The count had placed his son's estate in the best hands. Joyant undertook everything he could to increase the painter's fame. On his advice the family soon made their first endowments. For example in 1902, the Bibliothèque Nationale in Paris received a complete collection of printed graphic works including important test prints, and in 1904 the museum in Toulouse received four of the artists' pictures.

The greatest act of friendship which Maurice Joyant did Henri de Toulouse-Lautrec was the foundation of the museum dedicated to him in Albi in 1922 which with over 200 paintings, approximately 150 drawings and around 100 lithographs possesses the most important collection of Lautrec's work.

"Lautrec is more than a work," Émile Schaub-Koch acknowledged in 1935 in his "Psychoanalysis of a Modern Painter. Henri de Toulouse-Lautrec": "He is a vision. He means sagacity and distinct sensitivity. He is a state of mind who penetrated the hearts of his contemporaries and lives on in our whole generation as much through the technique which is wonderful enough as through his extraordinary spirituality. Like all great visionaries Lautrec is a precursor. He remains as fundamental as Baudelaire."

ILLUSTRATIONS

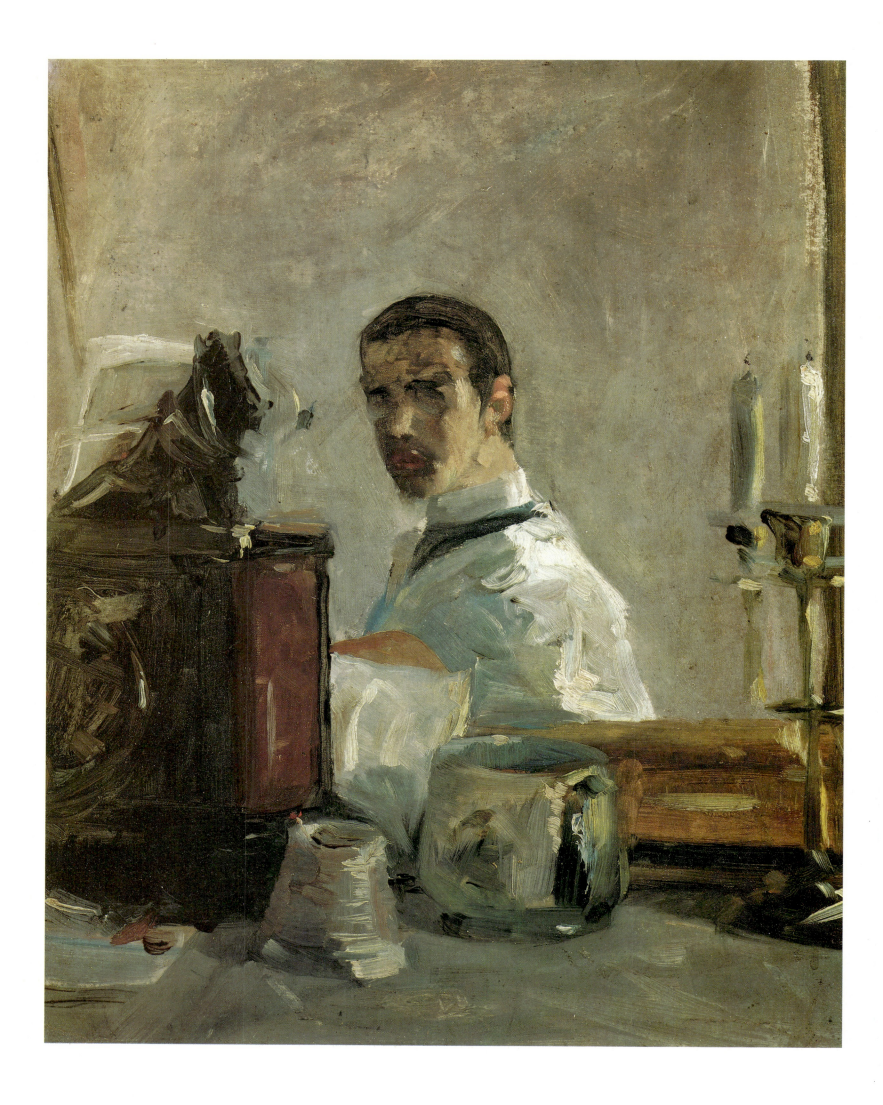

a n Fruit
Flankey

38

47

48

52

58

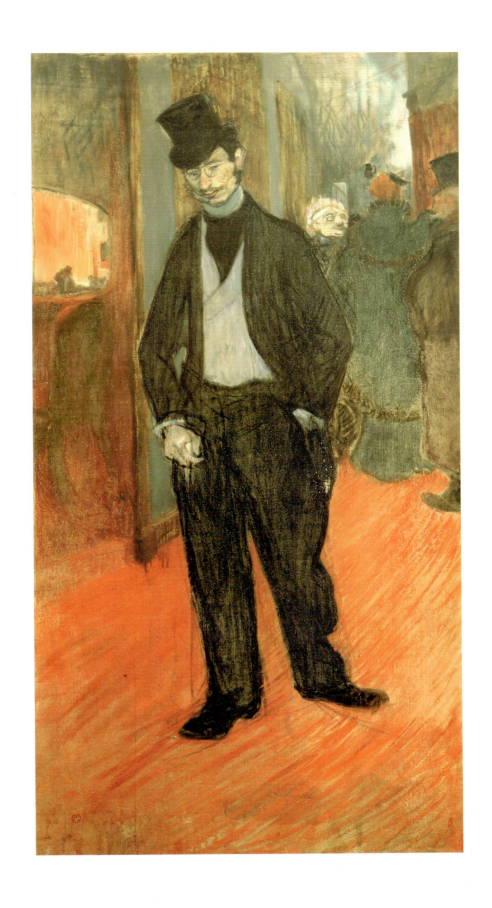

68

69

76

TREIZE LITHOGRAPHIES

par

H. de Toulouse-Lautrec

LIST OF ILLUSTRATIONS

94	The Amazon and Her Dog. 1898 Lithograph, 28.1 x 23.5 cm
95	Madame Réjane. 1898 Lithograph, 29 x 22.1 cm
96	In the "Star", Le Havre. 1899 Lithograph, 45.9 x 37.3 cm
97	Mademoiselle Cocyte. 1900 Watercolour on top of pencil on paper, 62 x 48 cm Musée Toulouse-Lautrec, Albi
98	In the "Rat Mort". Ca. 1899/1900 Oil on canvas, 55 x 45 cm Courtauld Institute Galleries, London
99	Messalina between Two Extras. Ca. 1900 Oil on canvas, 92.5 x 68 cm Collection E. G. Bührle, Zurich
100	The Milliner. 1900 Oil on wood, 61 x 49.3 cm Musée Toulouse-Lautrec, Albi
101	Le Margoin, Mademoiselle Louise Blouet. 1900 Lithograph, 32 x 25.8 cm
102	May Belfort. 1889 Lithograph, 29.5 x 24.2 cm
103	Cléo de Mérode. 1898 Lithograph, 29.3 x 24 cm
104	In a Café in Bordeaux. 1900—1901 Black crayon, 48 x 62 cm Musée Toulouse-Lautrec, Albi

The publishers wish to thank the following picture archives and museums for allowing the use of the following pictures:

Photographic acknowledgements:
Artothek J. Hinrichs Planegg: pp. 26, 83
The Bridgeman Art Library, London: pp. 43, 60, 68, 76, 92, 98
Bildarchiv Preußischer Kulturbesitz, Berlin: pp. 61, 69, 85, 86, 93, 103
Kunsthandlung W. Wittrock: pp. 46, 48, 53, 54, 55, 56, 62, 63, 64, 71, 72, 78, 79, 87, 94, 95, 96, 101
Musée Toulouse-Lautrec, Albi: pp. 29, 30, 31, 45, 70, 77, 80, 104
Ashmolean Museum, Oxford: p. 36
Wadsworth Atheneum, Hartford: p. 52
Musée d'Orsay, Paris: p. 57
Collection E. G. Bührle, Zürich: p. 99
Kunsthalle, Bremen: Table I, Table II
Staatsgalerie Stuttgart: p. 102

Where no other source is stated, the photographs are from the Berghaus archive.